W9-AOR-031

DISCOVER DOGS WITH
THE AMERICAN CANINE ASSOCIATION

I LIKE
COLLIES!

Linda Bozzo

It is the Mission of the American Canine Association (ACA) to provide registered dog owners with the educational support needed for raising, training, showing, and breeding the healthiest pets expected by responsible pet owners throughout the world. Through our activities and services, we encourage and support the dog world in order to promote best-known husbandry standards as well as to ensure that the voice and needs of our customers are quickly and properly addressed.

Our continued support, commitment, and direction are guided by our customers, including veterinary, legal, and legislative advisors. ACA aims to provide the most efficient, cooperative, and courteous service to our customers, and strives to set the standard for education and problem solving for all who depend on our services.

For more information, please visit www.acacanines.com, e-mail customerservice@acadogs.com, phone 1-800-651-8332, or write to the American Canine Association at PO Box 121107, Clermont, FL 34712.

Enslow Elementary, an imprint of Enslow Publishers, Inc.

Enslow Elementary® is a registered trademark of Enslow Publishers, Inc.

Library of Congress Cataloging-in-Publication Data

Bozzo, Linda.

  I like collies! / Linda Bozzo.

    p. cm. — (Discover dogs with the American Canine Association)

  Includes bibliographical references and index.

  Summary: "Early readers will learn how to care for a collie, including breed-specific traits and needs"—Provided by publisher.

  ISBN 978-0-7660-3847-9

  1. Collie—Juvenile literature. I. Title.

  SF429.C6B69 2012

  636.737'4—dc22

2011010474

Future editions:

Paperback ISBN 978-1-4644-0121-3

ePUB ISBN 978-1-4645-1028-1

PDF ISBN 978-1-4646-1028-8

Printed in the United States of America

012012 The HF Group, North Manchester, IN

10 9 8 7 6 5 4 3 2 1

To Our Readers: We have done our best to make sure all Internet Addresses in this book were active and appropriate when we went to press. However, the author and the publisher have no control over and assume no liability for the material available on those Internet sites or on other Web sites they may link to. Any comments or suggestions can be sent by e-mail to comments@enslow.com or to the address on the back cover.

Every effort has been made to locate all copyright holders of material used in this book. If any errors or omissions have occurred, corrections will be made in future editions of this book.

Enslow Elementary

an imprint of

Enslow Publishers, Inc.

40 Industrial Road

Box 398

Berkeley Heights, NJ 07922

USA

http://www.enslow.com

CONTENTS

IS A COLLIE RIGHT FOR YOU?

Collies are large dogs. They like to be with people and other dogs. They love children and make sweet pets.

A collie with long hair is called a rough collie.

A collie with short hair is called a smooth collie.

Collies are great pets for children.

Puppies are full of energy! Can your family keep up?

A DOG OR PUPPY?

Puppies are cute and love to play. But teaching puppies good manners takes time. Puppies need more attention than older dogs. If you do not have time to train a puppy, an older collie that is already trained may be better for you.

LOVING YOUR COLLIE

Collies enjoy lots of hugs. They are playful and like to learn new tricks. If you like to play with dogs, you may love owning a collie.

Collies love to play!

Running keeps your collie healthy.

EXERCISE

Collies need to exercise often. You will need to take your collie for a long walk every day using a **leash**.

Collies love to run. Some collies even enjoy swimming!

FEEDING YOUR COLLIE

Dogs can be fed wet or dry dog food. Ask your **veterinarian (vet)**, or animal doctor, which food is best for your collie and how much to feed her. Dogs need fresh, clean water every day.

Remember to keep your dog's food and water dishes clean. Dirty dishes can make her sick.

Do not feed your dog people food. It can make her sick.

Your new dog will need:

a collar with a tag

a bed

a brush

food and water dishes

a leash

toys

13

Brush your collie often to keep her fur looking nice and clean.

GROOMING

Collies will **shed** a lot. That means their hair falls out. They need to be brushed several times a week. They should be bathed with a gentle soap when needed. The soap should be a special one made just for dogs.

You also need to clip your dog's nails. A vet or **groomer** can show you how.

WHAT YOU SHOULD KNOW

It is hard to teach collies not to bark. They do not like to be left alone. This dog does not do well in hot weather.

Collies can live about twelve to sixteen years.

Make sure you can take care of your collie for many years.

You will need to take your new dog to the vet for a checkup. He will need shots, called vaccinations, and yearly checkups to keep him healthy. If you think your dog may be sick or hurt, call your vet.

A GOOD FRIEND

Your collie will need you to love and take care of him. The more time you spend with your collie, the happier he will be.

FUN FACT:
The famous dog
Lassie was a collie.

This is a poster for a Lassie movie. Lassie also had many TV shows and books.

NOTE TO PARENTS

It is important to consider having your dog spayed or neutered when the dog is young. Spaying and neutering are operations that prevent unwanted puppies and can help improve the overall health of your dog.

It is also a good idea to microchip your dog, in case he or she gets lost. A vet will implant a microchip under the skin that contains your contact information, which can then be scanned at a vet's office or animal shelter.

Some towns require licenses for dogs, so be sure to check with your town clerk.

For more information, speak with a vet.

This collie has one blue eye and one brown eye. You can find many great dogs at your local shelter or rescue group.

groomer—A person who cuts a dog's fur and nails.

leash—A chain or strap that connects to a dog's collar.

shed—When a dog's hair falls out so new hair can grow.

vaccinations—Shots that dogs need to stay healthy.

veterinarian (vet)—A doctor for animals.

Books

Green, Sara. *Collies*. Minneapolis, Minn.:
    Bellwether Media, 2010.

Paley, Rebecca. *Dogs 101*. New York:
    Scholastic, Inc., 2010.

Rake, Jody Sullivan. *Collies*. Mankato, Minn.:
    Capstone Press, 2008.

Internet Addresses

American Canine Association: Kids Corner
<http://acakids.com/>

Janet Wall's How to Love Your Dog: The Collie
<http://loveyourdog.com/collies.html>

INDEX